THE CHINESE INSOMNIACS

PREVIOUSLY PUBLISHED WORKS

Poetry:
  For the Unlost (1948)
  The Human Climate (1953)
  The Animal Inside (1967)
  The Shade-Seller: New and Selected Poems (1974)

Criticism: (With William R. Mueller)
  The Testament of Samuel Beckett (1966)
  Ionesco and Genet: Playwrights of Silence (1968)

Lectures:
  From Anne to Marianne: Some American Poets (Library of Congress)
  The Instant of Knowing (Library of Congress)
  One Poet's Poetry (Agnes Scott College)

Fiction:
  A Walk with Rashid and Other Stories (1979)

THE CHINESE INSOMNIACS

~NEW POEMS

Josephine Jacobsen

University of Pennsylvania Press
PHILADELPHIA   1981

Grateful acknowledgment is made to the following for
permission to reprint material which appeared originally
in their publications:

Beloit Journal   Poetry Now
Bennington Review   Rye Bread
Boston Review   The Sydney-Hampton Review
Commonweal   Southern Poetry Review
Cornell Review   The Back Door
Crazy Horse   The New Yorker
Folger Broadsides   The Nation
New Letters   Widening Circle
Poetry   Yankee

The author wishes to express her great gratitude to The Dowell
Colony and to Yaddo, where a number of the poems were written.

Library of Congress Cataloging in Publication Data

Jacobsen, Josephine.
   The Chinese insomniacs.

   I. Title.
PS3519.A424C5   811'.54   81–40556
ISBN 0–8122–7818–6   AACR2
ISBN 0–8122–1120–0 (pbk.)

Printed in the United States of America

For Ricky

With gratitude

Contents

I PERSONAE

II POEMS

III NOTES TOWARD TIME

I PERSONAE

❧ The Chinese Insomniacs

It is good to know
the Chinese insomniacs.
How, in 495 A.D.,
in 500 B.C.,
the moon shining, and the pine-
trees shining back
at it, a poet had to walk
to the window.

It is companionable
to remember my fellow
who was unable to sleep
because of a sorrow, or not;
who had to watch
for the wind
to stir night flowers in the garden
instead of making the deep journey.

They live nine hun-
dred years apart,
and turn, and turn, restless.
She says her sleeve is wet
with tears; he says something difficult
to forget, like
music counts the heartbeat.

A date is only a mark
on paper—it has little to do
with what is long.
It is good to have their company
tonight: a lady, awake
until birdsong;
a gentleman who made
poems later out of frag-
ments of the dark.

ᕦ The Gesture

In winter the house, which sits on rock,
braced on a granite ledge,
is a web naked to shock;
a web of boards; eaves at the wind's edge.

Like wind the snow is shredded through nettles,
the rock humps huge under the granulate
sweep. Inside the house, the mouse rattles
rapidly in the lathes and the spider's mate

hangs by moonlight in the midst of her own construction.
The months' names then are northern January, February, March.
Dust grows out of itself, and the sun
comes, if at all, in a knife's shape, thin, very sharp.

When the wheels bring voices the house, breached and entered,
appears as constant in its steady office:
the shrunk spider is the spit of her progenitors;
no change is apparent in the generations of the mice.

Then comes that season blue and green and limber
when the humans laugh and eat; make love; go, come.
Summer by summer—long, long in the mouse's number,
a flash in the rock's—they count to their anonymous sum.

The voices are set, distinct, in the cave of all silence,
as the rose and green are set now on the apple's icy bark.
The rock is a pebble's flash in the earth's summer;
the earth is a flash in the huge caves of the dark.

But something here rips out of its sequence,
will not feed and follow the sum of the mouse and the spider,
the rock. It is a gesture; a specific, chance
gesture. It belongs without end to its lover.

✺ The Rock-Plant Wife

The rock-plant wife is dead.
She failed to overwinter.
Along with the rare peony and most
of the candy-tuft
she is gone.

A cell bloomed in her body,
one icy night, hoped in her warmth
and was not disappointed;
sent its seed along her flesh,
its garden; like clover
took over that small space.

Now she herself is planted like a bulb.
Three of my friends are down there since first snow,
in that great soil where roots and rocks
and friends lie turning
with my turning world,
but do not turn to me.

The rock-plant husband moves among the rocks.
He could not keep his wife or peony.
He sends his spade into the shallow mound
for my dwarf-iris clump
and says her name to me
while friends of mine turn
silently in deeper soil.
I touched them, and they, me. We had
kisses and arguments and silences, all different.
Now I have the last.

The clump is up,
blue as our summer day.
He, like any gardener,
believes in spring. I simply say
(*pace* the gardener) in summer—
spring is too far.

Reading Aloud at Dusk in Spring

The small blind cripple's face was ready;
raised to receive the host of Mrs. Eddy.

Before the narrow house was tender dusk.
The dahlia-colored cat called Cheops licked his chops,

came into the room to the wheelchair and its dapper
sitter magnificent and fragile as a grasshopper.

A flower alive, with an African name, grew noiseless
in a pot near my hand that held the printed voice.

I read how matter, how sin, is nothing, is not,
and Cheops unbuttoned his eyes behind my back;

the orange tom's squint face lit that dusk like a moon,
but the blind clear eyes stared straight through that room;

the blind clear eyes went forth to battle matter,
to liquidate the mantel the pain the table the terror.

Never made flesh, the pure word rang like steel,
the corrupt clock tocked its tick and darkness fell.

A single rollerskate scoured the street and hushed;
the dark full violet rumpled its flowery flesh.

Pinned down in blackness, bright as a butterfly's flicker
she plunged her gleam like a knife in the void of matter:

washed with Mary Baker's smile the crucifix
to cleanse the shadow from the empty sticks.

⟋ℛ Mr. Mahoney

Illicitly, Mr. Mahoney roams.
They have him in a room, but it is not his.
Though he has become confused, it is not in this.
Mr. Mahoney cannot find his room.

A young blond nurse gentles him by the elbow.
I hear her again in the hall: "Mr. Mahoney,
this isn't your room. Let's go back and see
if you've brushed your teeth. Yours is *820.*"

Why brushing his teeth is the lure, I cannot say.
Does he prize it so? She darts on white feet
to spear him from strange doors; I hear her repeat
with an angel's patience, "Yours is down *this* way."

But 820 is a swamp, a blasted heath.
A dozen times returned, he knows it is wrong.
There is a room in which he does belong.
He has been to 820; he has brushed his teeth.

Before his biopsy, the harried nurses attest,
Mr. Mahoney was tractable in 820,
though very old and brown. He will have to go;
this is not the hall, not the building for his quest.

Tranquilized, Mr. Mahoney still eludes.
At 2 A.M. in my dark 283
the wide door cracks, and sudden and silently
Mr. Mahoney's nutty face obtrudes.

It is gently snatched back by someone behind it.
"That is someone *else's* room. Yours is this way,
Mr. Mahoney." He could not possibly stay.
He is gone by noon. He did not have time to find it.

❧ Pondicherry Blues

(for voice and snare-drum)

Mrs. Pondicherry was/ fat and mean,
she had four/ pug/ dogs and a limousine
black/ as West Virginia coal;
and she troubled herself about her soul,
yes, she surely was concerned/ about her soul.

Father O'Hare was thin as a steeple,
the poor and the lonely were his passion and his people.
Pondicherry would ask/ that man to come to dinner
and talk/ to him/ about The Sinner.
And Father O'Hare got very/ very/ tired of Mrs. Pondicherry,
he got raw-/ bone/ tired of Pondicherry.

She changed her will like/ she changed her furs
cause she surely did know that they both were hers,
and she drove that man beside himself
with her wills/ and her pelts/ and her pugs/ and her pelf,
she drove him purely beside himself.

One day she was sitting on her velvet seat
her mink/ round her shoulders and her footstool for her feet
and a cushion for/ each/ pug;
and her heart gave a leap and she fell on the rug,
she fell/ right/ down/ on her big/ red/ rug.

They put her into/ bed and called Father O'Hare
but he couldn't get there and he couldn't get there
and she lay on her bed for a/ solid/ hour
and she didn't say a word cause she didn't own the power,
didn't own the power to say/ a single word.

Her mind was thin and cold as a hag,
in her eyes was a beggar with a/ bowl and a rag,
and her ears/ heard/ a cold/ wind start
to blow the trash round the alleys of her heart,
to blow/ cold/ trash round the gutters of her heart.

But Father O'Hare he was/ serving the poor,
he never reached the house and he never crossed the door
till she closed her eyes and/ she stopped her breath
in the lonesome/ slum/ of death
that dark/ trashy/ street of/ death.

❧ The Arrivals

My dead are shining like washed gold.
Like gold from what-you-will freed:
cobwebs, mold, rust, the anonymous mud—
and plunged in the icy waver of water
to flash at the hot sun.

They come shining happily inside a moment
translated only now so long after.
They arrive in the comfort of comrades and a
nimbus of silence.

Accurate and able they shine
in ordinary glory
cleared from the clock's confusion that held them
distant, aghast.

❧ Elective Affinities

What a curious rendezvous: through mean sleet
down this straight street over corrupted snow
you travel travel to me. We never meet.

Shrilled from the dream of ease at this outrageous hour with a jolt,
when even cold schoolrooms sleep, you mine the dark
to sling your anti-gospel at my double-bolt.

What wretched congress: I light the sacred flame
under the coffee, listen, shiver in my wool,
and *Slackk!* comes the missile in this insane game.

You will miss your sleep, hate me, be stupid though not innocent:
or, industrious, you will be honored by the Horatio Alger Club
which says you will grow up to be our President.

Like a terrier I am on my diet of silliness and rape,
of murder most detailed; of a page of the dead's living faces:
a Buyer, a Broker, a Rotarian, and a Landscape-

Architect, who will buy, broke, rotate,
or scape nothing further. Someone is led away
in handcuffs. I spill coffee on a Head of State.

I don't even know your name. "Your Morning Eagle boy"
says your Christmas card, five days in advance,
wishing me, via a Lamb, all Peace and Joy

now, and in the New Year. In which, you'll be back
and I'll lie in wait for what we'll both have learned
that will alter ourselves, before tomorrow's *Slackk!*

❧ Carney Elegy

(For John)

The Indestructible Girl spun on a wheel:
she was not ugly, and looked destructible enough,
flattened and flying; and the Fire Eater, her young man,
ate fire: flames shot like promises between his lips.

The Barker barked, but silent as the tiger
they spun and blazed—the single silent tiger,
carrying his flame deep in his eyeballs and shallow on his hide;
the chic zebra, silent in his stripes.

And near us, and silent too, death, conventionally invisible.
The straw burned dusty under hoof and heel, the sun sucked motes
into the air to turn there and burn. We amicable
three, between the Barker and the fusty tent.

If that third member, if the guest, had spoken,
what should we then have said to one another:
Goodbye? I love you? Or both?
No more than whirling girl, fiery boy, tiger, zebra, straw,

New Hampshire July stubble, did we speak—to each other, that is.
As for love: this was our closest moment, or so I now say.
As for goodbye, my vanished circus friend—did the Fire Eater
say that, to the Indestructible Girl?

❧ Country Drive-In

Sudden around the curve a high-up and huge
face luminous as a clock blocks out a quarter-sky.
Small I move small in my small car below
the head of a giantess, unbodied as John's
on the screen's charger.
Blue as seas, its eyes release bright pools,
kidney-shaped tears slide down the vasty cheeks.
The lips' cavern parts on teeth
whiter and bigger than any bedded wolf's.
How can I fit her mammoth grief
into the dark below my matchstick ribs?

❧ Linkwood Road

The old lady walking, wears gloves. It is a shady
93 and the dogs' tongues drip. The old gentleman under
the dazed tree wears a jacket and, yes, a vest, and shined
black shoes. It is enough to break out flags about.

Surely they must die, of sunstroke, one, and of suffocation, the other.
In the meantime, what a fury of purpose and coolness:
who would trust the surgeon-of-crisis, in shorts?
Unthinkable the *corrida,* without the suit of lights.

It is doubtful that the old lady has a fitting destination;
the old gentleman is reading the obituary of a younger friend. That
white glove can be seen in the private dark, lessening its confusion,
and the jacket is comprehensible to the threatening mirror,
      and to all matadors.

ᔍ The Fiction Writer

Last night in a dream
or vision or barrier broken
strange people came to me.
I recognized them.

Some I had made, I thought.
Still they were strange—fuller, somehow—
with indistinct objects ahead of their steps.

Others who looked at me invitingly,
but threateningly too,
I had not seen.
Familiar though they were.

In his arms, in hers,
each carried a secret.
All were self-lit, like fish
from deepest water.

Nothing told me then
if I were bench or dock.
Only, *cousin, cousin, cousin*
said my blood, circling.

❧ Margins of Choice

The doomed gunman, surrounded,
arranges
his ammunition within reach, uses
his knees in the best way, adjusts his range.

The gardener cuts all the flowers, heaps
colors;
carries them off under the killer
frost's moon eye,
to die warm.

The man dying alters his pillow's angle,
shifts his gaze,
motions "no" with his finger, lays down
that hand; shuts, opens
his eyes.

So, as death quiet as the scent
of earth
moves closer, armed
with his only weapon,
separation,

I close with you, touch your skin,
your lips;
wake earlier, or lie awake,
look at you, look;
allocate
my instants'
shadowy heap.

✒ The Travelers

Up from the city street, as in any green wood,
the leaves came out, the red sun sank and died.
On that spring evening we breasted as we could
the brutal breakers of the decibel tide.

There was a lady, and a gentleman, there
at opposite ends of the room, unintroduced,
discrete, who, some of us knew, would make a pair
on a common trip before the leaves were loosed.

She managed a martini with finesse,
he shielded a gin-and-tonic from the smother;
no one elbowed through that press
to bring one up to face the other.

We, uncommitted, felt the isolation
of landlubbers who meet the sea:
joined in our minds by their common destination,
they seemed apt for travelers' company.

But at the very quay, which would go
first aboard, in what style, with what commissions,
delays, friends—no one could truly know
with certainty; not even their own physicians.

The Leopard-Nurser

Since children hear what they will hear, I heard
a man had gone to nurse the leopards.
"Women go?"
I asked, and "yes" they said, marveling
in admiration. I envied more than I admired.
Ah! the speechless hurt great leopards
in their woe.

I would go. In a round starry cave
of leaves and moss the green-eyed patients lay;
some worse
than savaged, some bloody, some unmarked:
each beautiful, fluid and fatal
to all save me, their skilled
and speechless nurse.

Though I grew up and went my daylight ways
I never lost that cave. I learned,
at secret length,
that any pain, or any love, reminds me:
a leopard-nurser's is a *métier*
by which a child nurses a dangerous beast
to strength.

II POEMS

ᵒᵍ The Gondolas

All night the gondolas knock
knock softly lightly like a hand
secure in its message. Under the windows, down
in the dark
the black gondolas knock softly.

Noon hushes the hand.
Pigeons flung into the sun they darken
glitter, break into fragments, fall
to fold their flight and stepping, stop;
the lion stares, all stars and wings, but stands;
the sumptuous banners move out and up
in the wind's hand;
flowing palazzi's peaks
shimmer and stream, their colors melt and flow
the bridges arching down melt under prows
the clouds confuse them as the bells
melt all their metal in the summer air.

At night the echoes echo echoes:
now you hear
the slight slap, ageless,
below sealed doors,
the soft quasi-silent slap
of water on the dank green sides of stone,
on the soft brilliant moss of footless steps.
Down black still ways palazzi go, deeper
than last night, into sleep.

The lights' cold broken flash
catches an orange peel, a stir of dark:
the soft slight slap jostles the gondolas
the black long empty gondolas
stir, knocking lightly
with a light hollow knocking
like a confident hand.

❧ Good Fortune of Pigeons

(For Arthur Gregor)

There is a dead pigeon hung
upside down in the bare big tree.
Around, about, flying out, in,
sideling, shooting their necks,
claws curved for balance,
conversing
steadily in soft glottals, are perhaps
a hundred pigeons.

Over wine and bread, a jug of daffodils,
inside the open window
we watch. Spring is still invisible
but the air is full of it, boiling in boughs.
We are shocked at such poise.

Why not another tree? Or at least
a decent distance? But no, all around
murmur and clean themselves
the wise and terrible pigeons,
saying, in throaty pigeon English:
Never mind.
Never

mind.

❧ The Provider

The night the flowers were butchered
I was gone.
Some sort of harvest comes
to everything nurtured.

But now who has the flesh, the wine
for days grown harder?
Out of this larder
will frost drink, and dine?

Now that his butcher's glance
stores blackness and pallor
will he swallow raw color?
Gnaw on fragrance?

I was not there; but have known
this slaughter, of old.
I know quite well the night, cold;
the knife, honed.

↬ The Things

My mother's gold serpent bit its tail.
Its tiny rubies stared along its back
to the flat gold head that held themselves.
All gold, and meaning forever.

Lopsided in red chalk, still the heart
under the feet is pierced by a smudged
red crooked arrow: clearly meaning
impacted pain, or pleasure.

Thing made word—blameless uncheating
speech: clear as those hasty sticks
the soldier crossed and held, high
in the rosy smoke for Joan.

ఆ There She Is

Standing in air
as bright as water
waiting for me
to pass.
How she can wait.
I know there is no
hope I can pass and find her gone.

Or of entering her room.
It is brilliant, distinct,
books on its shelves.
The books! What on earth,
my earth, do they say?
"Go get a book"
I tell her.

She comes back with a tiny smile
that lifts my lips,
and holds up an open book.
My book is a translation!
She holds up hieroglyphics:
the original.

She will receive anyone, anyone at all.
No one is too ugly, too sad,
too beautiful.
She plays absolutely
no favorites. If I held up
Holofernes' head
the hair of a head
would be clenched in her fingers.

What has she done with the others?
My friends who went into
that deep room of hers?
The dead, who stood

shoulder to shoulder with her
where she stands alone.
The distant; are they happy?

Let me see her bring them
to her side,
now:
coming forward,
smiling,
touching their hair.

∿ The Dream Habitués

Odd we've never met there,
spending all that time.
But then, it's a big country.

Erratic, too, as to lighting and climate.
Will it be crowded,
or the reverse? Tiresome, as to entry?

Yet I keep going back. God knows how often,
if I added up. Which means
I ought to know a fair-

sized group. But the people move about so.
And total strangers accost you,
looking familiar.

And the transportation!
Take you off to see a ruin, or cave,
and forget you. That's at its worst.

Yes, I've had incidents
curl the hair on my head.
But then at its best

how marvelous . . . I had a dance
there once more like, well,
swimming? or flying? No. Nothing I'd learned.

A couple of bad experiences.
And one doesn't know,
so to speak, which way to turn,

But then that can happen—
or something almost like it—
in any city. The closest shave.

And, if one wishes,
one can always wake.
Or, so far, I have.

~ Two Escudos

I

THE FADO SINGER WINGED IN BLACK

like The Lodger or a vertical bat,
black in the green light
sings of death and love
of love and treachery, of lonely death and love.

These are conferred on us, trivial
and happy drinkers, unconsumptive, wed,
having, all, return tickets to somewhere
and convivial presumptions. Taller
we rise as one to agree to his offer.

The fado singer handling our bones and nerves,
fingers our heart and finds it alive:
so he tells us we will die, or love will,
or the one come from the other;
or we will kill each other, or lose each other.

The fado singer must be right: truth truth
by the prick of thumb and fall of heart.
Something is left out, or added?
But there is more truth than lies.
Saurian lodger from the known room, black bat,
you can't hear my brave bat-voice cry, Garbled!

II
PHRASES IN COMMON USE

I have brought the phrase book. The rain has stopped,
wind makes the grass glitter and wink.
It is early: e cedo. And early in spring, too,
brown lambs and almond buds. The sun like a flute
stands the bare black vines on their tails, the snaky vines rise up

forked, black and bare.
My love, it is early. The bell bangs from the convent
on top of the hill
(all these Portuguese hills are blue as bluebells),
hear the flat sweet bang over the winking green:
e cedo.

Last night the phrases fell with the drops
in a dream of rain: the Phrases in Common Use.
A que distancia? Well, rather far. *Sao
horas de partir?* Not yet. Not really yet.
E tarde. And, if late and rainy,
then, *tenhio frio: I am cold.*
This is too hard: *I have bought
only a few things during my stay.*
And useful, but almost equally difficult: *I shall be glad
to help you, accompany you, invite you.*
And which to choose: *A culpa, (nao) foi minha:
it was (was not) my fault.*

This morning I understand that I do not need
to remember how to say any of that;
it is for later. And I have not yet learned to say

brown lambs, or *almonds.*
E cedo: it is early. Feel the sun.
Air moves the grass and drops flash in its green tangles,
the two mimosas blaze like a brace of angels.
E cedo: it is early. Venha ca: come here.
Prometo-lhe: I promise you.

❧ The Shell Eyes of Idols

What is it that terrifies about the shells for eyes?
Is it the bland stare? They stare—
a kind of confrontation, opalescent, fixed—
at, at. Yet they are blind,
turned inward; cast against a sea of light.

As eyes, they watch without motion;
as shells, they shine and block the glance.
Old as sight, almost as old
as blindness, they are the shells
of kings, eyes of the sea-king.

Brought up from blackness to refract
the light; they are polished by salt
and water, set in stone sockets.
The merciful blind close their eyelids.
Starers expect something: these gleam.

Lean, to shade their white look with your poise.
Turn. Look back at them. What they discover
with their brittle nacreous glare
is to endure. What they tell is
that shells are moved by the sea's breath,

that shells retain their messages;
tell stone sockets of a sea's motion.
These eyes, not shut, not open, lucent
and fixed, tell us eyes not shell
pass into each other, meeting.

~ Language as an Escape from the Discrete

I came upon two wasps
with intricate legs all occupied.
If it was news communicated,
or if they mated or fought,
it was difficult to say of that clasp.

And a cold fear because I did not know
struck me apart from them, who moved,
whose wasp-blood circulated,
who, loveless, mated, who moved;
who moved and were not loved.

When the cat puts its furred illiterate
paw on my page and makes a starfish,
the space between us drains my marrow
like a roof's edge. It drinks milk,
as I do; one of its breaths is final.

And even the young child, whose eyes
follow what it speaks, to see in yours
what it will mean, is running away
from what it sent its secret out to prove.
And the illiterate body says hush,

in love, says hush; says, whatever
word can serve, it is not here.
All the terrible silences listen always; and hear
between breaths a gulf we know is evil.
It is the silence that built the tower of Babel.

❧ Simon

I do what Simon says.
But the voice, quick and muffled,
gives some orders
which are not Simon's.

Simon I try to please.
It is necessary, and right, too, but
there is the doubt if
Simon has said, or has not.

Did Simon say, *Do that,* or
did that come Simonless
from the quick voice, the soft
instruction? Perhaps a bad mistake.

If Simon has not said it,
what then? Jumbled together: *Live, Die;*
which was authentic Simon? *Go. Come.*

Distinguish, Simon says.

∿ Tears

Tears leave no mark on the soil
or pavement; certainly not in sand
or in any known rain forest;
never a mark on stone.
One would think that no one in Persepolis
or Ur ever wept.

You would assume that, like Alice,
we would all be swimming, buffeted
in a tide of tears.
But they disappear. Their heat goes.
Yet the globe is salt
with that savor.

The animals want no part in this.
The hare both screams and weeps
at her death, one poet says.
The stag, at death, rolls round drops
down his muzzle; but he is in
Shakespeare's forest.

These cases are mythically rare.
No, it is the human being who persistently
weeps; in some countries, openly, in others, not.
Children who, even when frightened, weep most hopefully;
women, licensed weepers.
Men, in secret, or childishly; or nobly.

Could tears not make a sea of their mass?
It could be salt and wild enough;
it could rouse storms and sink ships,
erode, erode its shores:
tears of rage, of love, of torture,
of loss. Of loss.

Must we see the future
in order to weep? Or the past?
Is that why the animals
refuse to shed tears?
But what of the present, the tears of the present?
The awful relief, like breath

after strangling? The generosity
of the verb "to shed"?
They are a classless possession
yet are not found in the museum
of even our greatest city.
Sometimes what was human, turns
into an animal, dry-eyed.

ᕕ Winter Forecast

Let it be a consolation to you that nothing,
absolutely nothing, later, will be more frightening than the games.
Even the rules will not alter, even the sequence.
The people, yes. It is only the players who will not be the same.

In that dusk not quite late enough for rescue
by the calling voice from the room with the lamp lit,
the hidden hide, the seeker seeks. The seeker fears the hidden
and the hidden are rigid with terror of It, of It.

Bandaged and whirled, the blind man turns and turns;
and now in the stillest pond, the figures freeze in place,
though the blind white bandage comes and catches and bends
as the fingers walk and walk the anonymous face.

As now, the motionless sought know who is It,
in the still, still pond, in the fond hide-and-seek;
no more than now the hunter will fear the quarry,
the hider, the motionless, the terrible meek.

ᖇ Spread of Mrs. Mobey's Lawn

On Mrs. Mobey's lawn
Deer is near Squirrel,
who's neighbored by
Rooster; Black Man, Rooster's size,
all red lips and white eye-
balls stands also.

Speed is cast fast
in iron. Nuts are stored
in absentia. Squirrel
rears up solid; proud lust
treads only cut grass where
no hen errs.

Black small Man pops his look.
His lips and Rooster's comb
the same hard red.
Mrs. Mobey has flight,
providence, potency,
service, all arrested.

Faster than grass
grows Mrs. Mobey's lawn:
its iron-peopled stillness
advances acre by acre.
Deer, Squirrel, Rooster, Man
move iron towards us.

Rainy Night at the Writers' Colony

Dead poets stalk the air,
stride through tall rain and peer
through wet panes where
we sleep, or do not, here.

I know the names of some
and can say what they said.
What do we say worth the while
of the ears of the dead?

I know who shook marred
fruit of difficult bough
and from the rank discard
salvaged enough.

The rain stops; at two
the moon comes clear.
What they did, we know.
It is we who are here.

Naked under their eye,
we—honest, grave, greedy,
pedant, fool—lie
with what we make of need.

❧ Breaking and Entering

She turns from the priest
potent and humble:
between her teeth
God breaks and crumbles.

Fair enough. God eats her slowly:
senses, friends, powers;
attitudes, currents;
ah, hours.

She eats Him quickly, neat.
This is her body, and He in it;
what here she eats
breeds a live minute

to set against days
catatonic, demented.
Also, to rescue her
another love has entered,

humanly. Entries have sowed green
where ice held the fort.
She has broken love, been entered, seen
green in the desert.

She counts her life by such
breaking and entering:
understanding touch
as central to God, man, woman.

⮜ Ascetic's Soliloquy

How carnal the whole thing seems to the finer grain,
(aware how reliably flesh turns meager or shoddy,)
crude, to the sharp delicate filter of spirit and brain
that knows, in the longest run, how untriumphant is the body;

this exalting of supper at a crucial date,
this homage to appetite which, admittedly, always finishes
flat on its clown's face, now, or soon, or late;
this manic multiplication of wine, of oily fishes.

Spit, in the healing, blood, on the handkerchief;
and, after a resurrection, you would think
sticking a hand in a hole, a shabby proof.
Could such, reunited, do no more than eat and drink?

It has something to do, no doubt, with the common lot
(*common* being the operative word), the gross
degrading of the word, in the curious plot,
to a state, say what you will, of bizarre loss.

Well, let be the blood, spit, fishes of the story,
its strange dénouement, with cannibal overtones.
Well, let the battered, the carnal, the dying, munch on glory,
the marrow cry "soon, soon!" to the cooling bones.

How We Learn

Plurality in death
fogs our mind.
One man tries to breathe
in a sealed mine:
this is how we learn.
Eye to eye.

Corporate guilt, plague,
tidal wave, we make our
sluggish guess.
But the dead child in the ditch.
O yes.

At the siege of Stalingrad
an old man starving
ate his pet cat.
Later in the hall
hanged himself, because

after that meal
he looked around to find
all in its place;
his cat no longer there.
And he still was.

◈ The Monosyllable

One day
she fell
in love with its
heft and speed.
Tough, lean,

fast as light
slow
as a cloud.
It took care
of rain, short

noon, long dark.
It had rough kin;
did not stall.
With it, she said,
I may,

if I can,
sleep; since I must,
die.
Some say,
rise.

❧ Finally

Finally
the old woman saw

all things take back
their virtue

into themselves:

nouns swallow up
their adjectives;

the day's loose multitude
curl tight to now:

the whispering giant draw

into its acorn:
one ray compel

the starred abysses:
the gardens go into their

naked rose.

∾ Border

That country has never been her enemy.
She speaks its language, it uses hers freely.
Its flags make her heart lurch
and its music is indistinguishable from her desire.
Certainly, there are forests
only the crowns of which she has seen,
and a great river that keeps them green.

It is no reflection upon her that
she lacks a visa.
There is no visa.
Ambassadors come constantly
with a great variety of gifts;
blossoms and leaves.

She lives at its frontier, goes and comes
along its border, touching the great seal
with her hand.
The king comes over to sleep with her.

❧ Short Views in Africa

I

The elephant
comes past the Visitor two feet away,
watched through the blind's
chink. His shoulder strides,
he places like plush a foot,
then another.
The tufted tail goes by.

High up, at night, the Visitor sees
the herd come out:
singly, in moonlight, from the bush, the trees;
by twos; in a file of huge three;
scoop mud, blow, breathe. 103 elephants.

The Visitor
is healed by elephants,
pretends they will stay; falls asleep
kneeling at the sill. At four
the Visitor's eyes open:
the herd, rocking and shifting,
blowing, putting plashy feet,
is preparing to leave.
When the sun wakes her
they are somewhere else.

II

The best surprise is death.
She dreaded this
but it fits lightly. Even the frantic spurt,
ripped flank, snapped neck
settle so easily to: rock,
gold grass, stubble, bones, bones.

Everywhere, bones.
Simple, the bones of beasts.
This is the short view,
like a cut nerve—peace.
The bones are everywhere like grace
in the early sun.

III

The long, warped triangle
of the giraffe's pretty face,
the paintbrush lashes, the roving head
over the thornbush cruise, shy and leafy.
This air is pure with the ignorance of death.

Cat-lax the lion blinks
in noon's thin shade.
Lioness raises her head, stares,
lowers it; in a heap
the cubs are burrowed, dazed
with red food.

The skeletons inside the warm fur
go by paces, by springs, by stalks,

to their final sun;
to light, wind, grass.
Knowledgeable,
the Visitor watches the lions.

IV

In Olduvai are the bones
that block the way to ignorance.
Which bones, which minute first
looked on death and said, "That
belongs to me." Then said, then later said,
". . . belongs to what I love."

The Visitor can imagine herself—
imagines herself—
into the short sunny view;
bones unrelated, messageless,
the million bones benevolently whitening,
crying nothing
but hunger and motion;
not secretive of the permanent desire; not
saying
Mary Ann Kelly, Beloved.
Xenophon lies here.
I was Hannah.

V

Well. Bless the giraffe,
the elephant, the lioness, the short
blessed view.

Kneel at the window.
Wait under the thorntree
for the sun. Go away
carrying your difference, you cannot leave it.
Say, Not God
himself would dare to lay it on you without
relief.
Tell your secret bones: Wait.

III NOTES TOWARD TIME

❧ Notes Toward Time

I

The mad have nightmares. When
they wake
they find
their dream beside them.
Tense. But no present or past.

II

He cannot bear the dust's word.
She loves what dies.

What dies is unbearable
to her. What dies is what he loves.

The plastic rose
affronts. Only the falling

is bright. Falling
affronts. What goes was never true.

The rose affronts the light
by falling apart. Precious because

it falls, the rose rebukes
what stays.

The schizoid heart tells
what is alive, by its dying.

III

At a high inn in
a pinpoint angle near Trapani
in Sicily I came into

a cold room, this was dusk,
empty except for Miss
Judy Garland in a small brown box,
singing, singing
that's what I call
Balling
the Jack.

IV

A limited number of moons emerge.
Let us forget constantly that the planet's
turn is ours; our quiddity
begins and ends everything. Come here:
in our usual bodies, create the future and past,
bird and moon.

V

Help! While we slept débris has been emptied upon us:
blank hours like loops of undeveloped film
have littered us, a pile beyond belief; foxed chatter,
rusted conclusions, non-returnable affections. O the noise!
They will kill us, or anyway smother us from blue air.
There is a motion,
make it with me and we are elsewhere,
unscratched, silent as a leaf.

VI

In Erice stone is cold.
The usual angels tell the time by sun.
In the cold cleft the jackdaw tells the sun,
in the bronze cup the clapper tolls the moon.
Time stands between the angel and its angle.

The plastic rose is time's nightmare.
Take it in your hand, turn it
to petals fronting the light.
These stone garlands light the morning, empty the dusk.
The bare high country calls its seasons home.

The planet's motion holds the nest in stone,
the bronze bell tells the rose to fall apart.
Not numberless, our hours turn the earth:
the angel's eyes are blank, but in our sun
the stone sings, silent as a leaf.

A Motel in Troy New York

A shadow falls
on our cribbage. The motel window
is a glass wall down to grass.

A huge swan
is looking in: cumulus-cloud body,
thunder-cloud dirty neck

that hoists the painted face
coral and black. Inky eyes
peer at our lives.

It cannot clean its strong
snake neck. It stands
squat on its yellow webs

splayed to hold
scarcely up the heavy
feathered dazzle.

All of us stare. Then
in a lurch it turns
and waddles rocking,

presses the stubble to the tip
of the blue pond. Sets sail
in one pure motion

and is received by distance.
That crucial soiled snake neck
arched to a white high curve

received by distance
and the shadowy girl
across the water.

Bulletin from the Writer's Colony

Crack! The open
season is cracked
open. Birds?
Or is it deer?
That red in the wood
is not a leaf.

Today winter's dog, autumn,
snuffs through the leaves
ahead of his master;
who is ahead of his.

Inside these bounds, kept
to preserve elusive
other game, red-shirted
hunters do not hunt;

but from outside far off
red glints and goes
and the hollow sharp echo
holds for an instant in the air.

In the trees' leafy
bright recesses, in the stiff grass-
roots, the bird blood pounds and hushes;
the doe-eye stares:
Where? Where?

Here, after eggs and coffee,
dun hunters took off
for the jungle of the keyboard's teeth;
the canvas' riot of under-
brush; the pencil's secretive wood.

On the wall past hunters' formal
names are scratched
on plaques: kilroy,
le roi, was here.

Outside, the man through husks
of summer follows the dog; time
follows the man. The lucky
man's quarry dies.

But some bird breaks
to safety; a deer
clears the ground,
vanishes.

Here, if the hunt succeeds,
though time's trick over-
takes the hunter, his quarry
lives transfixed.

ᗌ Power Failure

The hard changes: concrete cracks and sprouts,
bulldozers eat their spinach and grow strong.
Asphalt's black plague ravages
where rubbish trucks cry, Bring out your dead.

Hastily the movie theater buries
its faces and gestures in the parking lot.
Six days alter the skyline. Five years build a stranger.
The manufactured blinds a frantic eye.

The pliant stays. The mango hangs itself
with fruity flowers and flowery fruit.
The tide runs very fast up over the rocks
making the sound of silk ripped,

and the sand blackens under the tide's shadow,
shines, pales before the tide comes back.
The oblique bat hunts down the lanes of dusk;
deep rainy valleys take the dark.

Last night the power failed. Below the moon
an Arawak, called back, could smell the island:
wind in its fronds; spice. And recognize its strong
shape under the gathered stars.

❧ The Clock

This stream of energy must be regulated . . . It is
done by a process of division. *The Book of
Changes.*

My clock jumped on cement.
The hands flew off.
Folded like yes
they settled at the bottom of the glass.
It was not dead.
I put it to my ear and tick it said.

It never stops. I wind
because it ticks.
It ticks because I wind;
its face is equal everywhere and blind.
It cannot mark
its light, separate its dark from all dark.

Though I was shrewd and knew
a thing or two,
lies lies it fed
me first: "salvation through division" what it said,
and gave to each
that identical portion no event could teach.

Love's lost extent, or fear's
gross minute
it equated.
That immaculate count related
figures to space,
both to its own unalterable base.

The hands agree:
we are in time;
even detached, believe
in synchronicity.
This handless clock and I have come
jointly to terms.

In joy and terror
I move in time where
nothing points to error;
I move in space
where love's event
and death's, notch
time's face.

❧ For Murasaki

Chrysanthemums
    come in spring too, now.
Force, again.

Unforced, their theme
    is autumn crisis
wet winds, cold sun;

summer's glowing
    death; the spicy
scent of formal fear.

Amethyst, sun-yellow, bronze
    chrysanthemums:
the big chilly heads

crisp and taut
    curl to the center
tight and tighter.

Or—small and stained, on
    earth-spattered sprays—
retain elegance.

Lashed to a poem
    like a petaled gloss,
they spoke for princes;

sprung from deep bowls
    at dusk in Paris
under the ruby lamp fringe:

send, forth and back
    in dumb color and scent,
Odette to Genji—

the chrysanthemum word.

ॐ Trial Run

But I think that things are the same with many
today as they were in Noah's time, when he built
the Ark of planks and timbers: for none of the
workmen and carpenters who fashioned it were
saved . . .

Piers Ploughman

They saw it take the water—the finished Ark,
after that long ridiculous procession:
the question-mark giraffe, the elephant
waving its ears, placing its plushy foot;
the loose-lip goat burning its yellow eye.
It floated, worthy, tight as you could ask.

Even where they watched, clotted on the top rocks,
would be a shining welter in, say, another hour:
not one green thing to clutch at as they went,
but water down upon them, up, to catch them—
the liquid howl of chaos, carrying
that tight right bark with all its procreant freight.

On the last sunny day (caulking the seams,
the green trees like a fleet of anchored clouds
above them; the crucial frame, the smell of shavings,
and the honor of accuracy, under the sweet blue
sky, paling, paling), they had understood
the only part of them to go would be the job.

It seemed unfair, but no more arguable
than the waters and the rough great wind.
And one, at least, just as the first cold hand

of water took his ankle, had a thought
that he would rather see her ride there, his,
still faintly seen, than, rocking in her hold

stand docile on commissioned planks.
She would bear it out, he knew, with bleat
and grunt and howl, and—doves being doves—
one might find out a green tree or its leaf.
In any case, it rode so as to argue
some future fortune for a carpenter.

Arachne, Astonished

In our porch rafters spiders spin
big webs that reach and tremble,
often with flies and sometimes moths hung in
the crosshatch of their dewy cables.

I cannot guarantee that friends will not die
or children put into practice what each learns;
but I thought that webs were a community
of architecture as unreconstructed as the fern's.

Space's amazed spider in her cage
is weightless. Fairly, one might expect her
to sulk in a daze, paw the air in arachnean rage
that good gravity monstrously should reject her.

Well, there are situations which ape
that of weightlessness; without guide-
lines, demand that thread from the guts take formal shape
while the cruelly uninflected voice says, "Improvise!"

O weightless, astonished Arachne, such
original alterations, situational spinning
of constructions! You frighten me very much.
Am I to understand, then, there is no end, none, to beginning?

~~ Food

A woman of the more primitive tribes
of Eskimo, concerned with nourishment,
cooked with heather clawed out from under snow;

mittens too precious, tore the heather loose
in that weather. The bare malformed hands,
nails curved, grew flesh like smoked wood.

Under an open sky, such fuel burned too fast;
in the snow-house, the walls would soften—
worse, smoke trouble the house's master.

She lay, low, to cook in a flat hut with a hole
in its roof. Blow! Blow! The ashes flew
into her mane, her red mongoose eyes.

To eat is good. To trap, to kill, to drive
the dogs' ferocity is heroic to tell:
full-bellied sagas' stuff.

The clawing for heather, the black curved nails,
cramped breath for smoke, smoke for breath,
the witch mask clamped on the bride face

bring nothing, but life for the nourished.
Poor cannibals; we eat what we can:
it is honorable to sustain life.

By her breath, flesh, her hands, no
reputation will be made, no
saga descend. It is only the

next day made possible.

❧ The Fittest

When the great dust
has settled, settled completely
and the air
completely is soundless,
he will be there.
In his neat thousands
will move.

Poor cockroach
he will be blind,
not sterile. His seed, his galaxy
of seed
will shine and rustle,
blind but agile.

Where a child's elbow
curved, where a man
spoke and moved
where bird and woman sang
will come his shining rustle:
where the rose
sprang from its green stem.

The Night Watchman

A small light, furtive, peers,
picks out a palm bole,
breadfruit green as a snake.
The night watchman is on his rounds, his right arm
heavy with its thousand years.

The dark keeps space behind
his left shoulder. For a moment
on my white wall in a white square
shadows of palm fronds struggle
with the invisible wind.

The Caribbean has taken back
its colors: the broken moon
scatters its steps on black. Here cocks
crow all night and dogs that slept
in the sedative sun, bark, bark, bark.

I ask of the watchman the seasoned
question: What of the night? From what
will he protect me? Other questions:
Where did she go? Is the mongoose
nocturnal? What should we have done?

Dogged as cock or dog, his light will return.
Protection! Protection? While
the thin knives of the clock
shred minute by minute, and the sea
turns over its bones?

ಶ It Is the Season

      when we learn
or do not learn
to say goodbye . .

The crone leaves that, as green
virgins, opened themselves
to sun, creak at our feet

and all farewells return
to crowd the air:
say, Chinese lovers by a bridge,

with crows and a waterfall;
he will cross
the bridge, the crows fly;

children who told each other
secrets, and will not speak
next summer.

Some speech of parting
mentions God, as in
a Dieu, Adios,

commending what cannot
be kept
to permanence.

There is nothing of north
unknown, as the dark
comes earlier. The birds

take their lives in their wings
for the cruel trip.
All farewells are rehearsals.

Darling, the sun rose
later today.
Summer, summer

is what we had.
Say nothing yet.
Prepare.

ᴄ᷾ᴠ Figure

Out of the bone landscape
of stone and sand, a man
on a burro appears

alone, distant;
egg for head, stick arms,
stick legs, out of all years

of the sand, the stone; going
to no seen spot, confers
a human form on the eye

before he vanishes
as though bony distance
had eaten him.

Nothing is like him. Vulnerable,
he has not profited
from the feral faunal data:

the yellow crab spider
on golden rod; the brown
beetle on soil; the katy-

did on its green leaf;
the delectable Viceroy
mimicking the acrid Monarch. Outwit,

or lie low and wait. The cock-
roach, in 300 million
years has not seen fit

to change. Yet durability
cannot be said
to be all. Nor fear.

The stony bony sandy view
shifted itself, focused
upon him till he left it there.